ETHICAL LIVING™

HUMANE

HOMES

CATHERINE ROBERTSON

Rosen
YA™

New York

Published in 2020 by The Rosen Publishing Group, Inc.
29 East 21st Street, New York, NY 10010

Library of Congress Cataloging-in-Publication Data

Names: Robertson, Catherine, author.
Title: Humane homes / Catherine Robertson.
Description: New York : Rosen Publishing, 2019 | Series: Living cruelty free: the guide to going vegan | Audience: Grades 7–12. | Includes bibliographical references and index.
Identifiers: LCCN 2017055272| ISBN 9781508180555 (library bound) | ISBN 9781508180562 (pbk.)
Subjects: LCSH: Animal welfare—Moral and ethical aspects—Juvenile literature. | Home economics—Moral and ethical aspects—Juvenile literature. | Veganism—Juvenile literature.
Classification: LCC HV4708 .R623 2018 | DDC 179/.3—dc23
LC record available at https://lccn.loc.gov/2017055272

Manufactured in the United States of America

CONTENTS

INTRODUCTION

Choosing a lifestyle that recognizes the value of all living creatures extends beyond what you eat. It also excludes, wherever possible, any form of animal cruelty or exploitation. If you want to support ethically created products made from animal-free materials, remember that those choices can be reflected in everything from the clothes and makeup you wear to what kind of home you want to live in.

The task of remaking your home with ethically made products in mind might seem pretty daunting. If you're living with your family, your home is probably already set up, with every room furnished and decorated. It's not as if you can throw everything out and start again.

The good news is that you don't have to. There are many small, gradual changes you and your family can make to an existing home that will make a big difference over time. Even if your family members aren't as vigilant about the types of products they use, they will still benefit from the changes you enact. Ethical living is about respect for the natural environment, so many changes that are cruelty free are also eco-friendly, which means they cost less because they use less energy. Your family can save money and do right by the planet, too.

However, if your family is building a new home, you have a responsibility to help ensure it's environmentally compatible. With the rise in awareness of what it means to be cruelty free and eco-friendly, it is becoming much easier to source other options. Businesses are offering humane, sustainable alternatives to the traditional products and materials we are accustomed to seeing. There might also be architects and builders in your area who understand

Look for local architects and builders who understand vegan principles and can help you create a cruelty-free and eco-friendly home.

these principles and can assist and advise you and your family.

To create a humane home, you'll need to know how to identify cruelty-free and eco-friendly products and how to make positive choices when buying home appliances, furnishings, and building materials and planning your home decor. You'll discover how to create a anticruelty garden and even how to trap bugs humanely. The vegan community is one source for resources and organizations that you can go to for more information and advice for all of this and more.

Changing your lifestyle to a more ethical one is a learning process. It's not about getting it 100 percent right all the time but about making the most informed choices you can and learning as you get started on your healthy, humane, and ethical journey.

Chapter One

WHAT MAKES A HOME HUMANE?

A humane home is one that doesn't have any animal-based products in it and doesn't contain animal matter in its building materials, furniture, soft furnishings (like drapes and carpet), and decorative objects. Sometimes it's obvious that something is made from an animal, but not always. Fortunately, there are many ways to find out, such as reading labels, asking specialists, and doing online research.

CRUELTY FREE AND ECO-FRIENDLY ARE NOT EXACTLY THE SAME

A vegan lifestyle is about having respect for every living thing on the planet, and vegans were among some of the first environmentalists active in promoting green alternatives. But it is important to all kinds of people to live in a house that is good for the environment.

Products that are kind to the environment are usually known as eco-friendly or green. However, not all eco-friendly products are cruelty free, as they may

contain materials made from animals or be sourced in ways that affect animals. You will need to ask questions and do some research before you make choices.

To be eco-friendly, a house needs to use energy (such as electricity) wisely, and preferably energy that is renewable. Nonrenewable energy comes from fossil fuels, such as coal and oil, and other sources like natural gas that will eventually run out, while renewable energy sources are able to regenerate and include wind, solar, and hydropower. Renewable sources of energy generally cause less air, soil, and water pollution, too.

It's important to many people that they live in houses that are kind to the environment and that use water and energy wisely, as does this house with solar panels installed on its roof.

The eco-friendly house also needs to conserve water and be built from materials that make as little impact as possible on the environment. To have a low environmental impact, the materials need to come from sustainable sources. Wood is a common building material, and it is sustainably sourced when the trees harvested are not endangered species and are being replaced with new trees. Cutting down trees without replacing them is called deforestation, and this practice has negative effects on the planet. It endangers the habitats of 80 percent of our land animals and plants, and it reduces the number of trees that play a critical role in absorbing greenhouse gases, which speeds up global warming.

Building products can also be eco-friendly when they are made from recycled materials, and they should be nontoxic and ideally biodegradable, which means they naturally break down without releasing toxins into the soil, water, or air. To live ethically, use products and materials that do not contain animal matter and are sourced in a way that does not hurt or exploit animals or endanger their habitats. You will need to look at both eco-friendly and anticruelty aspects when creating your humane home.

LEARNING FROM THE PAST AND FROM NATURE

Humans have been building houses for thousands of years, and many of the older construction

ASSESSING THE IMPACT OF PRODUCTS FROM START TO FINISH

A life-cycle assessment (LCA) is one way to find out how eco-friendly and cruelty-free a product is. It begins by looking at how the raw materials are gathered from the earth to create the product and ends by looking at what happens when all materials are put back into the earth.

In between, the LCA looks at how the raw materials are processed and the way the product is produced, manufactured, or assembled. It also reviews how the product is used, whether its use creates any waste or residues (especially ones that could be harmful), how long the product lasts, and what happens when it stops working and you need to get rid of it. At every stage, the LCA aims to capture the impact on the environment, which can include the impact on animals and their habitats.

To know how a product affects the environment from when its materials are sourced to when it is disposed of, ask about its life-cycle assessment.

Businesses are carrying out LCAs to help customers understand how their products compare environmentally with others on the market and to show their commitment to creating products that are eco-friendly. Some products have labels known as Environmental Product Declarations to show how they meet certain environmental standards. By knowing the life cycle of a product, you can understand how it's made and how it affects the planet, which will help you to make the most humane choices.

methods give us ideas today about how to make our homes eco-friendly and cruelty free. In the past, people had no option but to build naturally and sustainably. They had no artificial or synthetic building materials, and they couldn't afford or weren't physically able to bring materials in from other places, so they had to use what they could source nearby. They often needed homes that would withstand extremes of climate, such as great heat or frigid cold, and they wanted to avoid diseases caused by contamination of water or food supplies. Essentially, they had to find the best ways to keep themselves comfortable, healthy, and safe.

Mud bricks are one of the earliest building materials and are still widely used today, especially in regions with hot climates, like North Africa and Central and South America. In Latin America, buildings made from mud or clay bricks covered with heavy plaster are known as adobe. The bricks include mud or soil commonly mixed with straw, sand, and water, and their thermal mass makes the

home naturally cool in summer and warm in winter. Modern mud brick houses often have additional energy-saving features.

Cob is similar to adobe, except that the houses aren't made of bricks. Cob is a mixture of subsoil, straw, and water, with lime often added for extra strength. The mud or soil mixture is built up and formed into walls by hand, and it is a very simple and cheap way to build today.

In ancient Rome, architects developed building principles that highlighted the importance of positioning the house to receive the most benefits from the sun, protect it from wind and rain, and allow fresh air to circulate. Roman architects also looked at practices such as collecting and storing rainwater. Many eco-friendly homes today use rainwater tanks to conserve their use of water.

Early North American pioneers often used local materials to build their houses. Log cabins were sourced from nearby forests, and their sturdy, energy-efficient design is still popular all over the world.

Other modern forms of sustainable housing that look to the past for inspiration include the Earthship concept, which aims to be an entirely self-sufficient system, producing its own energy and food and processing and recycling its own waste.

Modern architects are also discovering how we can learn from animals and nature. Biomimicry looks at how living creatures capture, store, and use water and sunlight and how they process waste and regulate

Energy-efficient building methods have been around for centuries, and we can use them for inspiration when we're designing new humane homes, such as this self-sufficient Earthship.

temperature. Inspiration from nature helps benefit the environment. Among other innovations, the reflective content of spider webs that prevents birds from flying into them has been re-created in glass, and a new, less toxic wood adhesive copies the "glue" that mussels use to stick to rocks.

MYTHS AND FACTS

Myth: Vegans can't have animals, not even fake ones.

Fact: Vegans believe that animals should be respected and not hurt or exploited. So, a humane home would never display any stuffed real animals or keep animals, such as chickens or bees, for food. But many vegans share their homes with pets, favoring animals rescued from shelters over those from breeders, and have animal pictures, ornaments, and patterns in their furnishings and linens, although you won't find anything that looks like an animal hide. Use your judgment in your vegan home—if an image or object is respectful to animals, it's more than likely OK.

Myth: Your home has to be 100 percent vegan all over.

Fact: There are no "vegan police" who will come and check up on you, and even if you're building a home from scratch, it's hard to ensure every single item or material used contains no animal products whatsoever. Do your best to make informed choices, and try not to worry if your home can't be entirely cruelty free.

Myth: Nonvegan guests aren't allowed.

Fact: The expectations, if any, that you set for guests are entirely up to you. Nonvegan hosts might ask people to take their shoes off before coming inside or not to smoke, and most guests will be happy to respect those wishes. It might be hard to ensure your nonvegan guests don't wear leather or wool, but you can certainly ask them not to bring food with animal ingredients into your home. You can have fun explaining all the aspects that make your home cruelty free. Your guests may leave filled with inspiration to make their homes more humane, too.

Chapter Two

IF THESE WALLS COULD TALK

If your family is looking at building a new house or renovating the one you live in now, there are lots of ways you can make your home more humane and even completely cruelty free. As more businesses become aware of the benefits ethical living, it is easier to source all sorts of anticruelty alternatives to traditional building materials. Many ethically produced materials are also eco-friendly, which means they make better use of energy and have a lower impact on the environment. Your family can save money and be kind to the planet at the same time.

MAKE A MATERIAL DIFFERENCE

A humane home avoids building materials and fabrics made from animals or animal products or by testing on animals. These include materials made from wool, leather, suede, alpaca, angora, cashmere, mohair, calfskin, nubuck, and silk, and those that contain animal products, like bonemeal, feathers and down,

15

or fur. Read labels carefully or ask the seller, because some animal ingredients aren't easy to spot. Plastics can include animal fats and proteins. Glue can be made by boiling animal tissue and bone. Paints can contain milk, and paintbrushes can be made from animal hair. Using recycled car tires as a building material is a great way to recycle a product that's normally dumped, but some tires can include animal-based stearic acid, which helps the rubber hold its shape.

Materials you'll want to choose are those made from synthetic or organic compounds. Synthetic options include nylon, latex, polyester, polypropylene, down alternatives, rayon, and "natural" synthetics like modal, which is a variety of rayon sustainably sourced from beech trees. There's also rPET, or "recycled polyester," which is made from recycled pbuildinglastic bottles like the ones used for water. An alternative to wool insulation is mineral wool or rock wool, made from the residue that forms on the surface of molten steel during production.

Natural anticruelty building materials include wood, straw, paper, clay or mud, and products like fiberboard made from recycled paper. Fabrics include organic cotton, hemp, jute, sea grass, sisal, bamboo, linen, canvas, faux suede, corduroy, and "vegetable cashmere" derived from soybeans. There's even a fabric made from dried seaweed.

Unlike food and cosmetics, building materials and fabrics are not always plainly labeled as cruelty free or vegan, so be sure to ask questions before you buy.

There are plenty of cruelty-free and eco-friendly building materials. Ask your supplier what's best for your home in your quest to minimize its carbon footprint. This home in Kent, England, is carbon neutral.

TREAD LIGHTLY ON THE ENVIRONMENT

When your family is building or renovating, you will want to minimize the impact on animals and the environment. You can do that by looking at how you source your building materials, what size and style of building you choose, and how energy efficient the home will be. Sourcing materials locally is a great way to reduce your carbon footprint and support local businesses. It means fewer shipping miles, and you can check more easily whether the production methods

APPROVAL LABELS YOU CAN TRUST

Not all labels are created equal, so be sure your product's approval is from a reputable source. Here are some of the most well-known and respected labels for both cruelty-free and eco-friendly products. It's a good idea to double-check with the source organization that the product is displaying the trademark legitimately.

CRUELTY-FREE PRODUCT APPROVALS

The Certified Vegan Logo: The Certified Vegan Logo is a registered trademark administered by the Vegan Awareness Foundation. It is currently on thousands of products manufactured by more than eight hundred companies.

PETA approved: People for the Ethical Treatment of Animals (PETA) is an international organization that works for animal rights. It has around twenty-eight hundred cruelty-free companies on its searchable database.

Vegan Trademark: This trademark shows that a product has been assessed and approved by the Vegan Society. It will contain no animal ingredients or ingredients that have been tested on animals, and all processing aids used in the manufacturing process will also be vegan.

Leaping Bunny: The Leaping Bunny logo is an international symbol that identifies animal-friendly products.

ECO-FRIENDLY CERTIFICATIONS AND GUIDELINES

ENERGY STAR: This shows that a product meets a voluntary standard for energy efficiency administered by the US Environmental Protection Agency (EPA). The "star" rating label is on many household appliances. The EPA also administers the WaterSense water conservation standards and the Safer Choice product safety standards.

Look for recognized certifications for cruelty-free products and ratings like this one on household appliances that tell you how efficiently they use energy.

Forest Stewardship Council (FSC): The FSC certification logo can be found on wood and paper products and gives you assurance that they were sourced from responsibly managed forests.

GREENGUARD: GREENGUARD Certification is applied to interior products and materials that have low chemical emissions, which improves our air quality.

Green Home Guide: The US Green Building Council's Green Home Guide provides information, guidance, and recommendations about eco-friendly building products.

Green Seal: Formed in 1989, this was the first nonprofit environmental certification program in the United States. Green Seal provides environmental standards for numerous household and commercial goods.

(continued on the next page)

(continued from the previous page)

Green Label Plus: Green Label Plus is an independent testing program that identifies carpets, adhesives, and cushions with very low emissions of volatile organic compounds (VOCs) to help improve indoor air quality.

SCS Global Services: This organization used to be known as Scientific Certification Systems. It provides third-party environmental and sustainability certification, auditing, testing, and standards development.

are sustainable. Avoid materials that are rare or endangered, are not being replaced at the source, or are adversely affecting animals and their habitats. Reduce energy use by keeping the size of your home down. The average North American home is 2,600 square feet (242 square meters), which equals a lot of building materials and a high use of energy to light and heat it. You may not want to go to the other extreme and join the tiny house movement, with an average size of only 600 square feet (66 sq m), but make sure your home's size doesn't mean you waste energy unnecessarily.

PLANET-FRIENDLY BUILDING METHODS

Wood still has many advantages over more modern materials, such as concrete or steel. Trees absorb carbon dioxide, a greenhouse gas that contributes to climate change, and the processes that turn trees into building products are often less energy

20

intensive. Wood should always be sourced from well-managed renewable forests that care about maintaining biodiversity, such as those certified by the Forest Stewardship Council.

Hempcrete is a sustainable material made by combining hemp plant stalks, lime, and water into cement forms. It is easy to produce and use, nontoxic, and suits a wide range of climates because it has excellent insulating properties. Best of all, it has a negative carbon footprint.

A smaller house uses less building material and costs less to light and heat, so think about how big your home really needs to be.

Straw or hay bales are a by-product of farming. Excess straw is often burned, which contributes to the rise in carbon dioxide, so using straw bales in construction has an environmental benefit. Straw bales make excellent insulation and can be used in many typical house designs. They are even strong enough to create load-bearing walls. Straw bales are stacked as is or in a wood

21

frame, linked together by poles or an exterior mesh, and finished with a cover of stucco or plaster.

Mud or clay is an ancient but still efficient and cost-effective building material, particularly suited to hotter climates. Mud can be formed into bricks, which gives us adobe, or built up and formed into walls by hand, a method known as cob or rammed-earth construction. The mud or clay is commonly mixed with straw, sand, water, and sometimes lime. Mud's thermal mass makes it a great insulator.

Simple building materials like adobe, straw, and wood have been used for centuries and are still among the most cost-effective and energy-efficient choices around.

GO FOR LOW CHEMICALS AND TOXINS

Choose building materials with low levels of chemicals and potential toxins. It's healthier for you and every other living creature on the planet.

Natural materials reduce the use of petrochemicals, which are components in all sorts of common household items, such as carpets, televisions, detergents, paint, and many plastics. Petrochemicals are useful, but their manufacturing process is costly, uses a lot of energy, and is harmful to the environment.

Choose products with low levels of VOCs. VOCs can be released from solvents, paints, and glues as vapors or gases that can be harmful to your health.

Avoid materials that contain potentially toxic chemicals, such as the widely used formaldehyde; chromated copper arsenate (CCA), which is a pesticide/preservative; perfluorinated compounds (PFCs), which make materials stain resistant; phthalates or plasticizers, which make some plastics more flexible; and the flame retardants known as polybrominated diphenyl ethers (PBDEs).

Eco-friendly materials should deter moisture and mold, and you should be able to clean them with only natural, nontoxic cleaning products.

10 GREAT QUESTIONS TO ASK AN ARCHITECT OR A BUILDER

1. What building style or method do you feel would best support the creation of a humane home?

2. Are you able to source building materials that are cruelty free as well as eco-friendly?

3. Do you source your materials from local suppliers?

4. Are the natural materials you use from renewable and ethical sources?

5. Do any of the materials you use emit toxins or contain potentially harmful chemicals?

6. How will your choice of building style and materials help us use energy wisely?

7. What systems do you recommend for conserving water?

8. How will you incorporate vegan principles into our kitchen design?

9. How will you minimize waste during the construction process?

10. How can we be sure our home will last a lifetime?

Chapter Three

LOOKING AFTER OUR NATURAL RESOURCES

Ethical living is about respect for the environment, so when you're creating your humane home, you can look at ways to protect our natural resources. More efficient use of energy and water is better for your health and comfort and will cut down your household bills. Your family can save money and do right by the planet, too. Whether you're fitting out a new build or renovating, there are choices you can make that will enhance your home's use of energy and water and keep everyone in it happy and healthy.

STAY WARM, KEEP COOL, BE SMART

Creating a comfortable indoor temperature without raising the temperature of the planet is a priority. You can do your bit by choosing energy-efficient heating and cooling systems, monitoring your energy use, and making sure your home doesn't let any heat or cool air escape.

Before you buy a heating or cooling system, check its energy rating. There are several independent organizations that can tell you how energy efficient your system or appliance is. Look for labels such as the Environmental Protection Agency's ENERGY STAR rating—more stars means it's more energy efficient.

Eco-friendly ways to heat and cool your home include heat pumps and modern central air conditioner units (as long as they are connected to an efficient furnace and blower motor). Avoid nonrenewable and potentially pollutant fuels like coal and natural gas. If you source your wood locally, modern wood or wood-pellet burners can be energy efficient and carbon neutral, but they also emit fragments of soot into the air both indoors and outside, which can contribute to climate change and cause breathing problems.

Maintain your system regularly. Check any filters, seal all insulation

Modern wood burners can be energy efficient, but they also emit soot fragments into the atmosphere, which can contribute to climate change.

ducts, and get your system serviced by a reliable, reputable contractor at least once a year. Signs you may need to fix your system or upgrade to a new one include humidity problems, such as "weeping" windows, a lot of dust, or big temperature variations between rooms.

INSULATION IS ESSENTIAL

Insulation in your roof, walls, and subfloor is one of the most important factors in regulating temperature and using energy wisely. Avoid wool insulations and make sure your choice contains no animal products, such as animal glues, and isn't sourced in a way that affects animals or their habitats. If in doubt, ask your building specialist or supplier, or do your own online research.

Cruelty-free synthetic insulation options include mineral wool or rock wool, made from steel-production residue, and fiberglass (though this can sometimes contain formaldehyde). Natural options include straw bales, wood fiber, hemp, and cotton batts, made primarily from recycled industrial scrap. Insulation can also be made from plant-based waste materials such as nutshells, corncobs, and recycled corks. Often, these types of insulation need to be made thicker to ensure they have good thermal performance.

Plug those gaps, too, so the warm or cool air can't escape and you get the full benefit where you need it. Seal any leaks in windows with weather stripping, caulk, and draft-stopping tape, and if you don't have

Insulating your home is one of the best ways to ensure it stays warm and dry, and there are many excellent cruelty-free options, such as mineral wool.

double glazing, consider do-it-yourself window insulation kits. Use draft-stopping tape around doors, and lay a door snake on the floor. Most of these jobs you can do with your family, and for very little money.

WATER, WATER, WHEN EVERYONE NEEDS IT

Unless we live in a place that experiences regular droughts, we can take for granted that when we turn on a tap at home, water will come out. But even though 70 percent of the planet is covered by water, people can use less than 1 percent of it,

FREE AND EASY WAYS TO SAVE ENERGY

Switch off at the wall. Your appliances use electricity even when you're not using them. Your cable box alone can use up to half the energy of a modern refrigerator when it's on standby. Turn off lights when no one is in the room.

- **Open windows regularly.** This is a simple way to remove moisture and prevent damp and mold. When you're sleeping, leave your bedroom window open a crack to let out the moisture that builds up naturally over the night.
- **Dry your clothes on a clothesline.** Modern clotheslines don't take up much space and can often be folded away when you're not using them.
- **Draw your curtains at twilight.** This keeps heat in the house longer on cold days.
- **Keep underfloor vents clear.** Check that underfloor vents aren't being blocked, for example by plants. This makes sure damp air isn't trapped under your house.
- **Take shorter showers:** Just by shaving a few minutes off your shower time, your family could save quite a bit of money over the year.
- **Wash clothes on a cold cycle.** Hot washes can cost up to ten times more than cold, and modern washing machines and laundry detergents clean all but the dirtiest loads while using cold water.
- **Set your heater thermostat.** Aim for 65° F to 68° F for maximum efficiency.

and getting clean water to households is an energy-intensive process. As our population grows and the climate changes, water will become even more scarce.

29

Water is one of our most important natural resources, and we need to ensure that our homes don't waste a drop. Perhaps surprisingly, a ten-minute shower is more efficient than running a bath.

We need to use water more wisely than we do at present. The average home uses several hundred gallons of water each day, and we could use a lot less, and save money, by installing water-efficient appliances and having good daily water-use habits.

There are easy things you can start doing right away. Fixing leaky faucets is one. A faucet that drips at the rate of one drip per second loses 3,000 gallons (11,356 liters) of water a year.

Turn off the faucets firmly when you're not using them. Don't leave them running while you brush your teeth, and scrape food off your dishes before you rinse. The good news is that a dishwasher uses less water than washing by hand, but it's most efficient to only switch it on when it's fully loaded. If you don't have a dishwasher, use a small tub filled with as little water as possible.

Consider composting your food instead of using the garbage disposal. There are composting systems that can be used even in small homes. Clean and prepare vegetables in a bowl rather than under running water, and defrost food in a microwave.

When you and your family are building or renovating, check that your fixtures and appliances are water efficient. Look for the WaterSense labels, or ask your supplier or building specialist.

To limit the amount of water from faucets, install an aerator, which mixes water with air. A low-flow showerhead can save gallons every time you shower. The ultimate low-flow toilet is an outhouse, but fortunately, you can buy water-efficient indoor models these days. If you're really serious, consider a waterless composting toilet. Modern models are environmentally friendly and odor free.

SEEING THE LIGHT

The average household spends around 5 percent of its energy budget on lighting. Switching to energy-efficient light fixtures and bulbs is one of the quickest ways to cut your home's energy use and save money.

New lighting standards are now in place, and the old-fashioned incandescent bulbs that wasted lots of energy are no longer being made. The best options to replace them are CFL (compact fluorescent lamps) and LED (light-emitting diode) lightbulbs.

31

You can also buy halogen incandescents, but they are not as efficient as CFLs and LEDs.

These bulbs can cost more up front than the old incandescents, but because of the energy they save over their lifetime and the fact that they last a lot longer, they save you money overall.

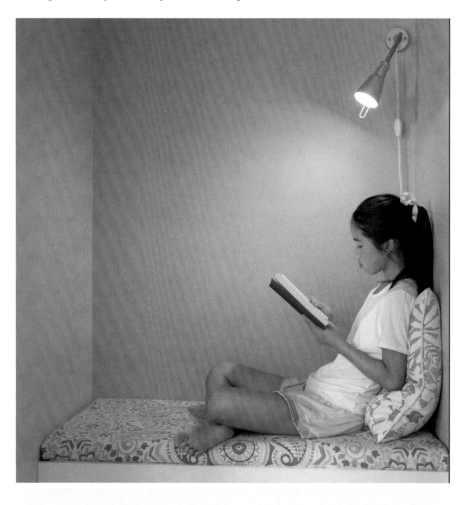

One of the best ways to save money on household power is to ensure that your lightbulbs meet the most current standards for efficiency.

LEDs are good for most general lighting around the house. They use 85 percent less electricity than traditional incandescent lightbulbs and can last more than fifteen times longer. They provide instant full brightness, and you can also dim them. Unlike CFL bulbs, LEDs don't contain mercury.

CFLs cost less than LEDs but can take a bit of time to reach full brightness. They're also good for general lighting around the house, particularly in rooms where the lights are left on longer, because frequent switching on and off can shorten their life. CFLs contain a small amount of mercury. Studies suggest this isn't a health issue, but to be on the safe side, avoid using CFLs in areas where they may be broken because special cleanup procedures are required.

Get the tech. With smart home apps, you can switch your indoor and exterior security lights—as well as your heating and appliances—on and off remotely. It could be an ideal way to monitor your energy use and make sure you don't use too much or waste any electricity. New apps are being launched all the time, so it's best to do your consumer research and check which one might suit your home.

Chapter Four

THE COMFORT OF KINDNESS

The finishing touches on your humane home are all about expressing your personality and creating an environment of comfort and enjoyment that also fits with vegan and ethical living principles. More businesses than ever are ready to help you use anticruelty products and provide compassionate alternatives to traditional animal-based materials. You can make kind choices without compromising on quality or style for all aspects of your decor.

BRIGHTEN YOUR WALLS

Modern wallpapers can be eco-friendly and cruelty free. Traditional wallpapers were made with vinyl, which emitted VOCs and contained chemicals that could encourage mold. So, if your home has old wallpaper, consider replacing it rather than painting over it, as mold growth can happen behind the paper. Look for wallpapers with no polyvinyl chloride (PVC) and no chemical coating or waterproofing. The best inks are water based with no heavy metals and low VOC emissions. The paper should be responsibly sourced and preferably certified by the FSC. The wallpaper should also be recyclable and manufactured in a way that minimizes emissions and waste. Avoid any glues or adhesives made from animal products. If in doubt, ask your specialist or supplier. There are nonpaper

Wallpaper is a great way to add color and personality to your home decor, and there are eco-friendly and cruelty-free options—some of which aren't even made of paper.

options, too, such as hemp, woven bamboo, renewable cork, jute, recycled wood, and sea grass. Most of these surfaces can be printed in patterns and colors, so your walls can be as bright or as neutral as you like.

Paint is a popular option and one that you can do yourself if you have the time. Go for water-based paints with low VOCs and low odor, which will be kinder to you and the environment. Avoid paints that contain milk, animal-derived glue, and acid casein, which is a by-product of cow's milk. Double-check that the paint has not been tested on animals and that its manufacturing process also excludes solvents and emissions. Choose your paintbrushes with care, as many are made from animal hair or fur; there are vegan brushes made from synthetic fibers that last longer and are less prone to breakage. They can also give a more consistent coverage and are easier to clean. Look for companies that minimize the amount of waste they create while manufacturing paints and papers and that sell their paints in recyclable tins and packaging.

TREAD LIGHTLY ON THE PLANET

A humane home needs floor coverings that are not made from wool, fur, animal hair, or animal skins of any kind. There are plenty of comfortable, quality synthetic carpet options, and you can also look at natural fibers, such as jute, sisal, and sea grass. Attractive rugs in all sizes are available in cotton, hemp, sisal,

36

and jute, as well as synthetic materials, like nylon and acrylic. Choose the styles and patterns you like and the ones that best suit the level of foot traffic in a particular area.

If you prefer hardwood floors, make sure the wood is FSC certified. Reclaimed wood is another option, and salvaged wood can be very attractive, too, as long as it does not contain any toxins from old paint, solvents, or sealants. With all floor coverings, make sure any sealants or adhesives are low VOC. Bamboo flooring is an option that resembles wood. Bamboo is a grass that is durable and easy to install and maintain. You'll need to make sure it is sustainably harvested and preferably locally sourced. New linoleum isn't the same as the old vinyl flooring, but rather is a natural covering made from a mix of renewable linseed oil, cork dust, tree resins, wood flour, pigments, and ground limestone. It is biodegradable and antibacterial.

Cork is a renewable natural option that usually comes in tiles. Cork trees are not cut down, and the harvested bark grows back every three years. It can be great for people with allergies, because it does not absorb dust or pollen. It also contains suberin, a natural insect repellent. Glass tiles made from recycled wine and beer bottles can be a beautiful option, and they also work for bathroom and kitchen walls. Glass tiles don't absorb moisture, which prevents mildew and mold. They won't stain, so they're easy to clean.

Natural materials like cork make durable and eco-friendly choices for floors. Cork does not absorb dust or pollen, so it's ideal for people with allergies.

PART OF THE FURNITURE

It's easier than ever to buy stylish, quality vegan furniture pieces, as well as soft furnishings, like drapes, cushions, and bed linens. You can avoid all forms of wool, leather, suede, hide, silk, and anything trimmed in fur or feathers, and instead buy pieces made from cruelty-free and eco-friendly materials.

Choose furniture pieces stuffed with materials like poly fiber, natural latex, or foam rubber and covered in durable natural and synthetic fabrics, like organic cotton and linen or polyester. Make sure the furniture's manufacturing process is eco-friendly and that the piece doesn't contain any animal-based glues or wool or down stuffing. Look for natural jute webbing. Avoid finishes or polishes that contain beeswax or animal fats, and go for alternatives like natural linseed oil. Eco-friendly finishes and materials don't include chemicals like fire retardants and are low in VOCs. Ideally, the pieces should be made from locally sourced materials. It's even better if those materials are recycled.

A note about faux leather, or vegan leather: this is a leather substitute, and it can be made from a wide range of materials, including cork, barkcloth, glazed cotton, waxed cotton, and paper. It is most commonly made from PVC or polyurethane. All PVC-based fabrics contain phthalates, which can be toxic, and solvents are often used with polyurethane-based faux leather. If this worries you, then ask the seller about the furniture piece's faux leather manufacturing process.

Instead of silk for curtains, cushions, or sheets, choose a bamboo silk alternative, organic cotton, linen, or any synthetic fabrics, such as rayon and polyester. Many retailers now offer down-free bedding and pillows, as well as cotton or synthetic-fiber quilts, blankets, and comforters, so you can avoid wool or animal hair.

When it comes to art, you will know what you like. If you want to have pictures of animals or ornaments in animal shapes, then you can. Taxidermy, though, is clearly harmful to animals. A humane home would never display any stuffed real animals. However, there are vegan artists creating "faux taxidermy" out of nonanimal materials,

Faux or vegan leather is a cruelty-free substitute if you like the look of leather, but ask about its manufacturing process to ensure it doesn't contain any toxins.

like wood, paper, plaster, and beads, which can be fun and attractive. It's OK to have animal patterns in your soft furnishings and linens, but use your judgment—if an image or object is respectful and kind to animals, then it will be suitable for your humane home.

CLEANING PRODUCTS THAT PASS THE WHISTLE TEST

There are many good cleaning products that are both humane and eco-friendly. Be sure to check that the

INSECTS INSIDE THE HOUSE: HOW TO TRAP THEM HUMANELY

Not too many people like having bugs, such as ants and cockroaches, inside the house, but all insects play a vital role in our ecosystem, so we should aim to preserve their lives as much as possible. Pesticides can be harmful to people and the environment, and traps are often cruel. For every insect killed, another will come inside, so it's better and more humane to find natural ways to discourage them from coming indoors in the first place. Ways to prevent insects in your home include:

- **Remove any sources of food and water:** Keep your dishes washed and your kitchen counters clean. Don't leave food out, including uneaten pet food. Take the trash out often. Plug up your sink and bathtub drains when you're not using them, and fix leaky faucets or pipes—cockroaches in particular are attracted to water.

- **Seal entry points:** See if you can find out where the insects are coming in, and seal up all gaps between floorboards, around windows and fuse boxes, and wherever plumbing passes through the walls and floors. Use caulking for larger gaps and nontoxic glue for smaller holes.

- **Repel insects naturally:** There are a number of safe, natural substances that you can use. Ants can be repelled by pouring cream of tartar where they enter the house and by cinnamon sticks, coffee grounds, chili pepper, cloves, dried peppermint leaves, and lemon peel and juice near openings. Cockroaches avoid dried bay leaves, so put some in your kitchen cabinets and drawers. There are nontoxic commercial products, but never spray these directly on an insect.

- **Put them back outside:** You can buy humane bug catchers for only a few dollars. These allow you to catch the insect and transport it outdoors without touching it.

41

approval label is from a reputable source and that the brand has the right to use that label. Not all manufacturers are honest.

To be humane, a cleaning product and all of its ingredients must not be sourced from or tested on animals. There are better nonanimal testing methods available, such as computerized models—find out what method your brand manufacturer uses. Avoid oils and polishes that include animal fats in the ingredients.

To be sure a product is eco-friendly, look for the Safer Choice label. This means that EPA scientists

When shopping for household cleaning products, look for a Safer Choice label to be sure a product is eco-friendly. Wegmans Food Markets won the 2017 Safer Choice Partner of the Year Award for their efforts toward the cause.

42

have evaluated every ingredient to ensure the product meets safety criteria for the chemicals, as well as sustainable packaging requirements and restrictions on levels of VOCs.

Be careful about products labeled as "natural." They typically use chemicals made from corn or other biological sources, instead of petroleum. But these still have the same chemical profile as petroleum, so they could potentially have the same impact on your health and the environment.

You might want to use all-natural cleaning products, like lemon juice, vinegar, and baking soda. They're readily available and could save you money.

Chapter Five

BIRDS, FLOWERS, AND BUTTERFLIES

Creating a vegan garden means encouraging birds, insects, and certain animals into your garden, while making sure you don't use any gardening products made from or tested on animals. You want to enjoy having a lot of life growing and buzzing around you, while respecting all living things on our planet. Many vegan gardens are also organic, which means they avoid all toxic sprays and chemicals and use natural methods to encourage growth and control insects and weeds. Even natural gardening products can contain animal-based ingredients. You'll want to avoid compost made from animal manure and fertilizers that include blood, bone meal, and fish emulsion.

START FROM THE GROUND UP

Great gardens need good soil, and there are natural ways to enhance the soil you'll be planting in. To be fertile, your soil needs nutrients. Nitrogen is especially vital if you're planning to grow vegetables. Without nitrogen, a plant cannot make the proteins and amino acids it needs to grow. Stunted plants are a sign of nitrogen deficiency. Nonvegan gardeners get nitrogen into the soil by using blood and bone fertilizer and animal manures, but there are more humane ways. You can plant crops that release nitrogen into the soil as they grow, such as legumes, clover, and mustard. You can also add coffee grounds and compost to the soil.

Lime corrects the pH balance in soil. If the pH is too high (alkaline) or too low (acidic), the plant can't absorb the available nutrients. Pale leaves and stunted growth are signs of lime deficiency. You can

Good soil packed with nutrients like nitrogen, potassium, and magnesium is the key to getting the plants in your garden to grow faster and better.

45

buy agricultural lime, which contains calcium, and dolomite lime, which also contains magnesium.

Potassium helps plants grow faster and resist drought, pests, and disease. It's hard to spot a deficiency unless it's major, when leaves will show brown spots or yellow edges. Natural sources of potassium are wood ash, either from a wood stove or bought commercially, and compost made from banana peels. You can also add seaweed for trace minerals.

COMPOST AND WORM POWER

Compost provides an amazing nutrient boost to any garden's soil, and it's easy to start your own natural compost pile with food scraps and other garden waste. A compost pile needs "green" or nitrogen-rich material, such as dry leaves and grass, corncobs and stalks, tea bags, and coffee filters. It also needs carbon-rich "brown" material, such as fresh grass clippings, vegetable and fruit peelings, coffee grounds, and flowers and cuttings. Don't compost animal products or poop, any weeds you're trying to get rid of, plants with diseases, or shredded paper, because it might have chemicals. Use pine needles and sawdust sparingly.

To help your compost break down quickly and release its beneficial microbes, chop larger items, and flip it or prod with a garden fork every one to two weeks to let air in. Keep its moisture level at around 50 percent. You can also give it a boost by adding alfalfa meal or comfrey leaves or buy some EM-1 solution, which is a special blend of naturally occurring beneficial microorganisms.

You'll know your compost is ready when it looks like dark, crumbly soil. You can use it as a fertilizer on your plants and lawn or as a potting mix. Compost also encourages natural worm populations, which is great for your soil. Earthworms digest the soil, add microorganisms from their gut, and excrete it as castings, which can contain up to ten times the number of nutrients as the original soil.

You can easily make your own nutrient-rich compost with food scraps and garden waste. Your garden soil will thank you.

PLANT LOCAL

Using plants native to your local area is an ideal way to ensure your garden works in harmony with nature. Not only will native plants thrive, but you can avoid the carbon miles that come with species that have to be transported. Also, because native plants are adapted to local soils and climatic conditions,

47

they rarely require the addition of fertilizer and are more resistant to pests and diseases than other species. The other major benefit is that native plants attract native wildlife. Birds and insects will come to the plants and flowers they know provide food and shelter. Depending on the size of your garden, you can consider leaving part of it wild or unmown. That will encourage native grasses and wildflowers to grow and become an even more attractive haven for wildlife.

The best places to buy native plants are your local nurseries and community plant sales. You can also learn about your state's native plant societies on the

Using plants native to your local area, such as the serviceberry bush native to North America, makes your garden much more likely to thrive and attract birds and insects.

48

North American Native Plant Society website or the Native Plant Information Network, which offers a comprehensive database of plants native to the United States and Canada.

Plants that attract birds are ones with seeds and fruit for them to eat or those that provide safe places for them to nest in, like climbing vines. Hummingbirds love nectar-rich flowers, such as red petunia, salvia, nasturtium, and fuchsia. If you love butterflies, you could plant flowers and allow wildflowers to grow, too, so the butterflies can lay their eggs. Popular flowering plants include butterfly bush, chrysanthemum, goldenrod, marigold, lilac, and lavender. Caterpillars need food, too, and plants they like include parsley, milkweed, and fennel. You don't need a big garden to create opportunities for bird and insects. Container plantings of native plants on doorsteps and patios, and even planting on roadside verges, can connect your garden with your local natural environment.

MANAGING CRITTERS YOU *DON'T* WANT

Some bugs and animals eat your plants and undo all your hard work. Luckily, there are ways to deter them that are kinder to all aspects of the environment. Strong plants are better able to resist insect attacks, and that means you need to keep your soil strong and full of nutrients.

For bugs like aphids, you can plant chives, marigolds, mint, basil, or cilantro. You can also place

GET IN THE SWIM WITH ANIMAL-FRIENDLY POOLS

If you live in a hot climate, swimming pools are a boon. But every year, countless animals, including frogs, mice, bats, and chipmunks, fall in and drown in pools or are poisoned by the chlorine. So, if you like to swim, here's how to make your pool safer for nearby creatures.

- Make a pool for animals: A pond that an animal can easily climb out of, such as one with sloping slides or rocks around it, may help divert them from your swimming pool. You can also use it to temporarily relocate any amphibians or water creatures you find in your pool.

- Fence and screen: There are lots of attractive ways to fence off a pool, which will deter animals from entering. You can even screen off the entire pool, while still allowing in the sunshine.

- Plant safely: Locate plants that attract bees or birds away from the pool area so they won't fall in.

- Give them a way out: You can buy flotation devices that give animals a safe place to crawl onto and ramps that will help them escape the water or the skimmer, if they end up there.

- Turn off the filter at night: Many animals are active at twilight or at night, and if they fall in while the filter is on, they can get swept into the skimmer. Filters are better used during the day to get rid of algae and residues.

- Help restore natural habitats: Animals like amphibians, who live in wetlands, often seek out water if none is available. Helping with wetland recovery projects can be as simple as minimizing your use of fertilizers to reduce pollutants and planting native gardens that can direct runoff into the soil, where contaminants can be filtered.

aluminum foil at the base of your plants, which reflects sunlight and scares the aphids away. Cilantro can also deter mites and grasshoppers, as can other plants like calendula. It's worth experimenting. Codling moths eat all pip fruits (or, several-seeded fruits such as apples and kiwifruit) and walnuts; you can try filling cheese-cloth squares with lavender, chives, garlic, or cedar chips. Slugs dislike mint, lemon balm, sage, pine needles, and parsley. Many insects do not like garlic, but be aware that homemade garlic sprays will also affect beneficial insects, including pollinating bees.

Deer can jump as high as 8 feet (2.4 meters), so fences are not always the best deterrent. Try creating a boundary by placing soap shavings or used cat litter on the ground. You could also hang a salt lick to distract them from venturing off the path into your garden. Natural rabbit repellents include thorny plants, yarrow, asters, lavender, and sage. An interesting option is to put oven racks around the plants, because apparently, rabbits don't like how they feel underfoot.

A LAST WORD ABOUT WATER

The average American household uses more water on its garden than it does on washing clothes and taking showers—almost 9 billion gallons (34 billion L) of water a day. Water is a vital resource that will only become scarcer as the population grows and our climate changes, so when you're creating your garden, plan how you will conserve water. One of the best ways to

Deer are beautiful, but they can wreak havoc in your garden, so putting down a salt lick can be a great way to distract them.

use water wisely is to install a WaterSense-labeled irrigation controller, which can save you thousands of gallons over a standard clock timer.

Think about your site, and choose plants that will easily grow. For example, don't plant sun-loving plants in shady areas. Native plants are used to your zone, so they will thrive with minimal water. Group plants together depending on how much water they need, so you don't overwater some plants and underwater others. Remember to conserve, think sensibly about your garden and building site, and have fun maintaining your humane home.

GLOSSARY

animal exploitation Humans using animals, often cruelly, for profit.

antibacterial Destroys or prevents the growth of bacteria.

biodegradable Naturally decomposes without releasing or leaving pollutants.

biomimicry Human-made innovations inspired by the natural world.

carbon emissions Carbon dioxide, the main greenhouse gas, that is released into the atmosphere.

climate change Long-term changes to the world's temperatures that most scientists believe are caused by the increase in greenhouse gases.

cruelty-free Does not hurt, exploit, or endanger animals or any other living things.

deforestation Cutting down forests, particularly native noncommercial ones, without replacing them.

eco-friendly Having low or no impact on the environment.

green Another way to say eco-friendly.

habitat The places where animals naturally live.

humane Having or showing compassion or benevolence.

life-cycle assessment (LCA) A way to assess the environmental impact of a product from start to finish.

nontoxic Not containing any toxins or poisons.

petrochemicals Chemicals made from petroleum and natural gas and used in many household items.

phthalates An acid-based substance used in solvents and to make plastics more flexible and durable.

raw materials The ingredients of any product before they are manufactured.

renewable energy Energy from sources that can replace themselves, such as wind, water, and solar energy.

sustainable A resource that is able to continue being used because it is replaced and not depleted.

synthetic Human-made and not natural.

taxidermy Stuffed, dead animals used for display and decoration.

thermal mass Materials that can absorb and retain a lot of energy are said to have high thermal mass.

vegan A person who does not eat or use animal products of any kind.

volatile organic compounds (VOCs) Chemicals released from products or materials as vapors that can be potentially harmful to health and the environment.

FOR MORE INFORMATION

Earthsave Canada
#170-422 Richards Street
Vancouver, BC V6B 2Z4
Canada
(604) 731-5885
Website: http://www.earthsave.ca
Facebook: @EarthsaveCanada
Twitter and YouTube: @earthsavecanada
Earthsave Canada provides advice about switching to a
    plant-based diet and lifestyle, advocating for compassion
    toward animals and environmental sustainability.

Environment and Climate Change Canada (ECCC)
200 Sacré-Coeur Boulevard
Gatineau, QC K1A 0H3
Canada
(819) 938-3869
Website: http://www.ec.gc.ca
Twitter: @environmentca
The ECCC focuses on conserving Canada's natural
    heritage, combating pollution, learning about climate
    change, and reducing household waste, with the aim
    of ensuring a clean, sustainable environment.

Forest Stewardship Council (FSC)
708 First Street North, Suite 235
Minneapolis, MN 55401

(612) 353-4511
Website: http://us.fsc.org
Facebook: FSC.US
Twitter: @FSC_US
YouTube: FSCUS
The FSC is an international organization working to protect plant and animal species and the rights of indigenous peoples by ensuring forests are responsibly managed and providing products sourced from sustainable forests with a recognized certification.

North American Native Plant Society (NANPS)
PO Box 69070, St. Clair PO
Toronto, ON M4T 3A1
Canada
(416) 631-4438
Website: http://www.nanps.org
Facebook: @nativeplant
Twitter: @tnanps
The NANPS helps restore healthy ecosystems across North America, preserving wild native plant habitats and bringing native plants back to populated areas.

Peta2
2154 W. Sunset Boulevard
Los Angeles, CA 90026
(757) 622-7382
Website: http://www.peta2.com
Facebook, Twitter, and Instagram: @peta2
Peta2 is the youth program of PETA, providing advice,

recipes, shopping guides, and other resources for young people who want to know about being vegan and making humane changes in their lives.

US Environmental Protection Agency (EPA)
1200 Pennsylvania Avenue NW
Washington, DC 20460
(202) 564-4700
Website: http://www.epa.govs
Facebook and Twitter: @EPA
The EPA protects the health of people and the environment, giving advice on being eco-friendly as well as information on how safe and efficient products are at using energy and water through its ENERGY STAR, WaterSense, and Safer Choice ratings programs.

US Green Building Council (USGBC)
2102 L Street NW, Suite 500
Washington, DC 20037
(800) 795-1747 or (202) 742-3792
Website: http://www.usgbc.org
Facebook and Twitter: @USGBC
The USGBC publishes the Green Home Guide, which has everything you need to know about "greening" your home, whether you're building or renovating.

FOR FURTHER READING

Askew, Claire. *Generation V: The Complete Guide to Going, Being, and Staying Vegan as a Teenager.* Oakland, CA: Tofu Hound Press, 2008.

Curley, Robert. *New Thinking About Pollution* (21st Century Science). New York, NY: Britannica Educational Publishing, 2011.

Curley, Robert. *Renewable and Alternative Energy* (Energy: Past, Present and Future). New York, NY: Britannica Educational Publishing, 2012.

Elliott, Melisser. *The Vegan Girl's Guide to Life: Cruelty-Free Crafts, Recipes, Beauty Secrets and More.* New York, NY: Skyhorse Publishing, 2010.

Fleischman, Paul. *Eyes Wide Open: Going Behind the Environmental Headlines.* Somerville, MA: Candlewick Press, 2014.

Gore, Albert, Jr. *An Inconvenient Truth: The Crisis of Global Warming: Teen Edition.* New York, NY: Viking Juvenile, 2007.

Newkirk, Ingrid E. *Making Kind Choices: Everyday Ways to Enhance Your Life and Avoid Cruelty to Animals.* New York, NY: St. Martin's Press, 2005.

Rafferty, John. *Climate and Climate Change* (Living Earth). New York, NY: Britannica Educational Publishing, 2011.

Sivertsen, Linda, and Tosh Sivertsen. *Generation Green: The Ultimate Teen Guide to Living an Eco-friendly Life.* New York, NY: Simon Pulse, 2008.

BIBLIOGRAPHY

Gowrishhankar, Vignesh, and Amanda Levin. "America's Clean Energy Frontier: The Pathway to a Safer Climate Future." September 2017. http://www.nrdc.org/resources/americas-clean-energy-frontier-pathway-safer-climate-future.

Kopalek, Michael, and Perry Lindstrom. "Natural Gas Leak at California Storage Site Raises Environmental and Reliability Concerns." US Energy Information Administration, February 1, 2016. http://www.eia.gov/todayinenergy/detail.php?id=24772.

Mann, Sarah E. "More Than Just a Diet: An Inquiry into Veganism." University of Pennsylvania, Spring 2014. http://repository.upenn.edu/cgi/viewcontent.cgi?article=1021&context=anthro_seniortheses.

Monahan, Patrick. "Veganism Could Save the World, New Study Argues." Science, April 19, 2016. http://www.sciencemag.org/news/2016/04/veganism-could-save-world-new-study-argues.

Moss, Doug, and Roddy Scheer. "The Safety of Carpets Made from Recycled PET Plastic." Scientific American. Retrieved October 12, 2017. http://www.scientificamerican.com/article/safety-of-recycled-pet-plastic-carpets.

National Geographic. "Deforestation." Retrieved October 14, 2017. http://www.nationalgeographic.com/environment/global-warming/deforestation.

National Resources Defense Council. "Water Efficiency Saves Energy: Reducing Global Warming Pollution Through Water Use Strategies." March 2009. http://www.nrdc.org/sites/default/files/energywater.pdf.

NASA. "NASA Study Finds Carbon Emissions Could Dramatically Increase Risk of US Megadroughts." February 13, 2015. http://www.nasa.gov/press/2015/february/nasa-study-finds-carbon-emissions-could-dramatically-increase-risk-of-us.

Reiny, Samson. "Rising Carbon Dioxide Levels Will Help and Hurt Crops." NASA, May 4, 2016. http://www.nasa.gov/feature/goddard/2016/nasa-study-rising-carbon-dioxide-levels-will-help-and-hurt-crops.

Reiny, Samson. "US Desert Songbirds at Risk in a Warming Climate." NASA, March 8, 2017. http://www.nasa.gov/feature/goddard/2017/us-desert-songbirds-at-risk-in-a-warming-climate.

Tabb, Phillip, and A. Senem Deviren. *The Greening of Architecture*. Surrey, England: Ashgate Publishing Limited, 2013.

US Energy Information Administration. "What Is Renewable Energy?" US Department of Energy, June 1, 2017. http://www.eia.gov/energyexplained/?page=renewable_home.

Zazzera, Joe. "How Biomimicry Is Shaping the Nature of Our Buildings." Smart Cities Dive. Retrieved October 12, 2017. http://www.smartcitiesdive.com/ex/sustainablecitiescollective/building-evolution-how-biomimicry-shaping-nature-our-buildings/134086.

INDEX

F

G

H

I

L

M

N

P

People for the Ethical Treatment of Animals (PETA), 18
perfluorinated compounds (PFCs), 23
petrochemicals, 23
phthalates/plasticizers, 23
polybrominated diphenyl ethers (PBDEs), 23
polyvinyl chloride (PVC), 34, 39

Q

questions to ask an architect, 24

R

Roman architecture, 12

S

Safer Choice label, 18, 42–43
SCS Global Services, 20
soil, maintaining
  lime, 45–46
  nitrogen, 44–45
  potassium, 46
straw/hay bales as building material, 21–22
swimming pools, animal-friendly, 50

T

toxic materials, 23

U

US Environmental Protection Agency (EPA), 18

V

veganism
  benefits of lifestyle, 4
  defined, 4
  as a learning process, 6
  myths and facts about lifestyle, 14
  reasons for, 4
Vegan Trademark label, 18
volatile organic compounds (VOCs), 20, 23

W

water, using wisely
  dishwasher, 30
  efficient appliances, 30
  fixing/turning off faucets, 30
  low-flow shower/toilet, 31
WaterSense label, 31, 52
wood as building material, 9, 12, 20–21

ABOUT THE AUTHOR

Catherine Robertson lives in Wellington, New Zealand, a country known for its beautiful environment. She is a published novelist with a master's degree in creative writing and has recently built a new house using eco-friendly principles. She is a conservationist, is a member of the New Zealand Green Party, and supports the humane treatment of animals. Both of her dogs came from rescue kennels.

PHOTO CREDITS

Cover YinYang/E+/Getty Images, (bottle logo) Alvaro Cabrera Jimenez/Shutterstock.com; p. 5 Tyler Olson/Shutterstock.com; p. 8 anweber/Shutterstock.com; p. 10 Dalibor Danilovic/Shutterstock.com; p. 13 IrinaK/Shutterstock.com; p. 17 G. Jackson/Arcaid Images/Getty Images; p. 19 Bloomberg/Getty Images; p. 21 ppa/Shutterstock.com; p. 22 Bill Florence/Shutterstock.com; p. 26 Arena Creative/Shutterstock.com; p. 28 Sergej Cash/Shutterstock.com; p. 30 Clay McLachlan/Aurora/Getty Images; p. 32 Pete Ark/Moment/Getty Images; p. 35 Steven Taylor/Photographer's Choice/Getty Images; p. 38 Portland Press Herald/Getty Images; p. 40 ChiccoDodiFC/Shutterstock.com; p. 42 Andriy Blokhin/Shutterstock.com; p. 45 Jamie Hooper/Shutterstock.com; p. 47 pryzmat/Shutterstock.com; p. 48 Stephen J. Krasemann/All Canada Photos/Getty Images; p. 52 S. J. Krasemann/Photolibrary/Getty Images; back cover, interior pages background pattern (leaf) mexrix/Shutterstock.com; interior pages background pattern (bamboo) wow.subtropica/Shutterstock.com.

Design and Layout: Tahara Anderson; Editor: Carolyn DeCarlo; Photo Researcher: Nicole Baker